GAMES
BABIES
PLAY

FROM BIRTH TO
TWELVE MONTHS

GAMES BABIES PLAY

FROM BIRTH TO TWELVE MONTHS

collected by

Vicki Lansky

Distributed to the book trade by
Publishers Group West
Emeryville, CA

BOOK PEDDLERS
MINNETONKA, MN

SPECIAL THANKS TO:
EDITORS CYNTHIA STANGE , KATHRYN RING, CAROL LOWRY,
AND CONTRIBUTORS, DAVID KATZNER, JEAN RUCHERT, TERRI
ELLIS, BETSY KOCH, RHONDA KOZIAK, AND SHARON PETERSON,
STACY AND ROY HASLETT.

COVER AND TEXT DESIGN: MACLEAN & TUMINELLY

COPYRIGHT © VICKI LANSKY 1993
FIRST PRINTING / APRIL 1993

Publisher's Cataloging in Publication
(Prepared by Quality Books Inc.)
Lansky, Vicki.
    Games babies play : from birth to twelve months / Vicki Lansky.
    p. cm.
    Includes index.
    ISBN 0-916773-32-9 (cloth)
    ISBN 0-916773-33-7 (pbk.)

        1. Infants. 2. Play. 3. Games.   I. Title.
HQ774.L3 1993   793'.019'22
                         QBI92-1441

BOOK PEDDLERS
15245 MINNETONKA BLVD.
MINNETONKA, MN 55345
612/912-0036

PRINTED IN THE UNITED STATES OF AMERICA

99 98   18 17

DEDICATION

In memory of

June Louin-Tapp, Ph.D.
1929-1992

Professor at the Institute of Child Development
at the University of Minnesota
and, more importantly a friend, who would have enjoyed reading and
commenting on this book had she had the opportunity.

TABLE OF CONTENTS

Introduction

3 TO 6 MONTHS MILESTONES 29

6 TO 9 MONTHS MILESTONES 51

9 TO 12 MONTHS MILESTONES 71

introduction

Welcome to the wonderful world of your baby.

In this first year you will see your baby's abilities expand as your little one grows and develops in amazing ways. There is no way more wonderful to share in this process than through the delight of play and games.

In baby play each family member learns about the other—and about oneself. You learn about attention spans, abilities, communications without words, patience, anticipation, crescendos, beginnings and endings, laughter, and the joy of touching.

And best of all, in playing games, a baby learns that he or she is loved.

Babies collect information through their senses. They need to have stimulation brought to them—stimulation to match their growing abilities. Here are activities to encourage as well as delight.

While these ideas are given in a loose chronological order, don't forget to go back and play the games suggested in the earlier chapters as your baby matures.

With all the newly developing skills that these games will help encourage, know that this is only the beginning. The best is yet to come.

Enjoy!

Vicki Lansky

BIRTH TO 3 MONTHS

Babies are a miracle of sensory development. Their eyes focus well only at around eight inches for the first month of life. Still, this allows them to concentrate on what's most important—studying their parents' faces and the faces of those who feed and care for them. Newborns also respond to bright colors, bright lights and objects put near their face.

Infants' hearing is comparable to that of adults. In fact, soon after birth, infants have been shown to prefer music they heard while in utero. They can be startled by sudden, loud noises. Newborns' sense of smell is developed enough for them to be able to identify their mother's smell.

In the first three months, a baby's energy is devoted to self-regulation in the areas of eating and sleeping. Still, they take in any information that acts upon them. Body movement is at first random and erratic. But each passing week brings more interaction with the environment, more smiling, and more control of those tiny hands which wave in front of baby's own face.

Neck muscles are not strong enough to support the head adequately so your help is needed for the first few months. A hand will grasp an object placed in the palm, though it is only a reflex action.

By the third month, babies have become social beings, eager to smile, clearly recognizing familiar people, and delighted with attention. The two of you can build a foundation of special, shared times by relating through games played together.

BIRTH TO 3 MONTHS

All Washed Up
Baby Firming
Baby Parts
Baby Pull-Ups
Bathtub Time-Out
Bed Bouncing Baby
Dance with Me, Baby
Exercycle
Finger Games
I'm Gonna Getcha!
Look at Me
Lost in Space
Lullaby Your Baby
Old World Traditions
Parent A Cappella
Playback
Pom Pom Play
Puppet Play
Rattles
Starburst
Stretchy, Stretchy
Strokes for Li'l Folks
Tickle Time Rhymes
The Tootsie Roll
Toy Target Practice
Who Do I See?
Wrist Watch

ALL WASHED UP

T alk and sing while bathing your infant in a sink or plastic molded tub. Sing about the parts of the body you're washing. The following can be sung to *"London Bridge Is Falling Down"*:

Head, Shoulders, Knees and Toes

Head and shoulders, knees and toes,
Knees and toes, knees and toes.
Head and shoulders, knees and toes,
Eyes and ears and mouth and nose.

Sing this to the tune of *"Here We Go Round the Mulberry Bush."*

This Is the Way We Wash Our Face

This is the way we wash our face,
Wash our face, wash our face.
This is the way we wash our face
On a *(day of the week)* *(morning or evening)*.

Other verses to include in your bath time routine are:
- clean our toes,
- wash our arms,
- scrub our feet,
—*this list is endless.*

These songs go well beyond infancy and will take on many variations as your baby learns the parts of the body.

BABY FIRMING

Your little one can help you get back in shape and make it more fun. Once your doctor okays your resuming exercise, there are firming-up routines you can begin that can include and entertain your baby.

Kissy-Kissies

With your baby lying face up on the floor, get on all fours over your baby with your baby between your hands. Begin gently by just lowering your head to kiss your little one. Advance to lowering your straightened body—with your weight resting on your knees and hands angled slightly inward—down to kiss your baby. Don't let your stomach sag or your back arch. Push back up and repeat. If you were able to do standard push-ups before you were pregnant, work gently back to this stage without straining yourself. If you don't like push-ups, limit yourself to "cat curls" where you just arch your back and then relax it again.

Better Bottoms

Lie on your back with your knees bent, feet on the floor, and baby sitting on your stomach with your hands securely around the torso under his or her arms. Squeeze your buttocks tightly together and raise your hip bones upward and hold for one or two seconds. Release and lower. Next flatten the small of your back to the floor and curl your head and upper body up while keeping your back straight on the floor. Release and lie back. Alternate these two routines to build up back and abdomen strength.

BABY PARTS

Your baby's body parts will provide the topic for many of the conversations the two of you will carry on as you interact. You'll find your newborn is not much of a conversationalist—most of the burden of small talk will fall to you. Your repetition of such words as "nose," "eyes," "fingers," "chin," and "ears" will start your baby on a lifelong learning process.

Knock, Knock

Knock, knock. *(Knock on baby's forehead.)*
Peek in. *(Open eyes wider.)*
Open the latch. *(Push up the tip of the nose.)*
And walk right in. *(Walk fingers into mouth.)*
How do you do, Ms. Chin-chin-chin? *(Wiggle chin.)*

Thumbkin, Pointer

Thumbkin, pointer, middleman big.
(Point to each of baby's fingers.)
Silly man, wee man, rig-a-jig-jig.
(Roll baby's hands around each other.)

Months from now, when your baby becomes well-versed in the names of the body parts, you can purposely slip in a wrong word or two so he or she can "correct " you.

BABY PULL-UPS

When your baby is two or three months old and can raise and hold up his or her head, you two can begin a wider range of games.

Infant Sit-ups

Lay your baby on the floor (or bed) in front of you , or in your lap facing you. Gently pull the baby up to a sitting position, while holding hands. Say something like, *"U-u-up you go,"* or *"Baby sits up now."* Even at two months your baby's head may still lag a bit when pulled to a sitting position.

Then slowly lower your baby back down. Say, *"Dow-w-wn you go,"* or *"Now Baby lies down."* Repeat until one of you tires.

Infant Stand-ups

At three months or closer to four months, lay your baby against a pillow facing you or sitting on your lap. Firmly grasp his or her hands and begin counting. Let your baby know what's coming so he or she can anticipate the excitement to come.

"Are you ready to stand up? Let's do it! One." (a long, drawn out count to build excitement.) *"Two."* (Begin to increase the tension.) *"Three!"* On the count of three, slowly pull the baby to a standing position. Keep a steady patter of conversation going to lend enthusiasm to the exercise. By four months most babies enjoy being upright and you'll feel your baby pushing down on you while in a standing position.

BATHTUB TIME-OUT

Treat yourself to a soothing bath with your baby, making bath time a cozy, relaxing playtime instead of a chore. *(Put the answering machine on first.)* Be sure the room is warm—heat it, if necessary, by running the shower on hot for a few minutes before or when filling the tub. Keep two large towels nearby. Put one on the rug outside the tub to place your baby on momentarily when lifting him or her in and out.

As the two of you enjoy the water together, sing to your baby. Sing your favorite pop tunes or Sinatra classics. Music creates intimacy and connectedness.

Even in the bathtub, you can rock your baby in your arms as you sing or hum. Or you can nestle your infant on your legs on your lap—and move with the music the two of you are making together.

Keep both of you submerged in the warm bath water as much as possible because the air always feels cool to a wet baby. Or consider keeping your baby wrapped in a light cotton diaper or light cotton blanket while in the water for that feeling of being "swaddled" that some babies prefer.

BED BOUNCING BABY

M otion is often soothing as well as entertaining for an infant. Lay your baby on your bed and gently bounce the mattress. *(If using a waterbed for play, never place a baby face down or leave alone; there's danger of entrapment and suffocation.)* If your baby enjoys that, help him or her to a standing position, supporting the rib cage with your hands. Gently bounce the baby so his or her knees bend. This motion should get your baby into the swing of bouncing. Even six months from now when he or she is old enough to keep balanced, hold onto hands and encourage this routine.

Certain songs lend themselves to this type of fun such as:

You Are My Sunshine

You are my sunshine, my only sunshine.
You make me happy when skies are gray.
You'll never know, dear, how much I love you,
Please don't take my sunshine away.

Variation: Another motion game enjoyed by newborns is a "ride" atop a washing machine during the wash and spin cycle while in an infant seat. Note, however, that a baby should NEVER be left alone during this "ride."

DANCE WITH ME, BABY

Dancing to music entertains and relaxes everyone. Babies love rhythmic movement, which becomes the basis for later walking, running, and skipping.

Turn on the music and let it move you. Ask your baby for a dance. Be it rap, rock, or melodic tunes, sweep your baby into your arms and dance away. Sing or hum the melody as the two of you sway to the music. After your dance, thank your partner and return your baby to a stationary location.

You can dance sitting down, too, by cradling your baby in front of you so you can look at each other while the two of you sway to the music.

Dance Little Baby

Dance, little baby,
Dance up high.
Never mind baby,
Mother (Father) is by.
Up to the ceiling,
Down to the ground.
Backwards and forward,
Round and round.

EXERCYCLE

B abies love to have their arms and legs moved for them, especially before they gain control of their own movements. A good workout helps your baby develop muscles and learn how to use them joyfully. And exercise helps everyone sleep better!

Hold the baby's feet and gently guide them in a cycling motion. You need only to remind a baby as this is a natural exercise. Once you've helped a baby "get in gear," your little one will try to carry on the game without help as he or she matures.

One appropriate song for this excercise is:

Row Your Boat

Row, row, row your boat
Gently down the stream.
Merrily, merrily, merrily, merrily,
Life is but a dream.

Variation: To help a baby practice kicking, hold a toy or cradle gym within range of the feet so contact can be made. *(See other exercises on page 22.)*

FINGER GAMES

F inger plays, with their recognizable patterns, quickly become favorites with your baby.

Here Comes Mousie

Running your fingers up the baby's leg, across the tummy, and into the neck area, combines the excitement of anticipation and the tickle. Let your voice pitch rise as the "mousie" approaches. "*Here comes mousie. Here she comes! She's going to get you!*"

Bumble Bee

Use your free hand as a buzzing bee while holding your baby. Make a buzzing sound as your index finger circles the air. The baby's eyes should be following your "bee." Build gentle suspense before landing the "bee"—with a slight tickle—on your baby. Next, take the baby's finger and help it circle as the "bee." Land it on your cheek. This game can continue until the "bee" tires. Or use this rhyme:

> Bumble bee was in the barn *(Circle finger in the air.)*
> Carrying his dinner under his arm *(Closer to the baby.)*
> Bzzzzzzzzzzzz. . . . . *(Poke baby.)*

Tickle Me

Using the word "tickle" allows your little one to anticipate playtime together.

> Tickle me, tickle me, tickle me, too,
> It's fun to be tickled because I love you!

I'M GONNA GETCHA!

Place your baby on the floor in an infant seat or on a blanket. Smiling, come closer to the baby, with hands outstretched. Say softly, *"Watch out, Jami. I'm gonna get you. Here I come!"* Build the excitement in your voice as you approach.

Gently grab your baby, while you say, *"Gotcha!"* in a bit louder voice. Laugh and hug him or her after each "gotcha," so the baby knows it's a game. Many parents and babies love it when "I'm gonna getcha" ends with mouth-contact blows on tummies and necks. Repeat several times, so the baby learns the pattern of this play.

If your baby is wary of this game, you might try having one adult hold her or him, giving "protection," while the other adult pursues. If your baby still shows any sign of fear or unhappiness, stop the game. The next time you choose to play it, be more gentle so the baby feels less vulnerable.

Once your baby is sitting up and is familiar with the game, you can approach from behind, calling softly, *"I'm going to get you! Here I come!"* As your baby begins to crawl, it becomes the basis for a game of chase.

LOOK AT ME

Once your baby's head control is good (usually two months or older), play time can add to strengthening those neck muscles.

Lie on your back, your baby lying face down and his or her head on your stomach. Sit half way up and rest on your elbows and talk to your little one, *"Look at me, look at me,"* giving a big smile. Your baby will lift his or her head to see you. Ten seconds or less is long enough at any one time in the beginning before you recline again so your baby can rest too.

Once your baby is stronger, place a small rolled-up towel under your baby's arms/chest in the same position on your stomach to practice and play *"Look at me."* Or move your baby off your tummy and onto the floor using the rolled-up towel under your little one and play variations of *"Look at me."* Coming from behind your baby, crouch to one side *("Jackie, look at me")* to encourage head-turning as you move from one side to the other side.

LOST IN SPACE

Make a fascinating visual toy to enjoy with your baby by filling a clear plastic soda bottle with water, a squirt of dishwashing liquid detergent, a few spoonfuls of cooking oil and a few drops of food coloring. Moving and shaking this colorful bubble bottle will delight and entertain.

LULLABY YOUR BABY

The slow, gentle, rhythmic sounds of lullabies have soothed parents and children in all cultures for thousands of years. A rocking song can bring both parent and child to a quieter place, where each can feel the harmony. Don't stop singing lullabies when your baby's no longer a newborn—just expand your repertoire of favorites.

Rock-a-Bye, Baby

Rock-a-bye, baby,
On the treetop
When the wind blows,
The cradle will rock.
When the bow breaks,
The cradle will fall,
And down will come baby,
Cradle and all.

Rock-a-bye, baby,
Thy cradle is green,
Father's a nobleman
Mother's a queen;
And Betty's a lady
And wears a gold ring;
And Johnny's a drummer
And drums for the king.

Kum-Bah-Yah

Kum-bah-yah, my Lord,
Kum-bah-yah.
Kum-bah-yah, my Lord,
Kum-bah-yah.
Kum-bah-yah, my Lord,
Kum-bah-yah.
Oh, Lord, Kum-bah-yah.

verses: Someone's singin', Lord,
Kum-bah-yah . . .
Someone's laughin', Lord,
Kum-bah-yah . . .
Someone's cryin', Lord,
Kum-bah-yah . . .
Someone's prayin', Lord,
Kum-bah-yah . . .

All Through the Night

Sleep, my child, and peace attend thee
All through the night.
Guardian angels God will send thee,
All through the night.
Soft and drowsy hours are creeping
Hill and vale in slumber sleeping.
I, my loving vigil keeping,
All through the night.

While the moon her watch is keeping,
All through the night.
While the weary world is sleeping,
All through the night.
O'er thy spirit gently stealing,
Visions of delight revealing,
Breathes a pure and holy feeling
All through the night.

Sweet and Low

Sweet and low, sweet and low,
Wind of the western sea,
Low, low, breathe and blow,
Wind of the western sea!
Over the rolling waves we go,
Come from the dying moon and blow,
Blow him again to me;
While my little one, my pretty one,
Sleeps.

Sleep and rest, sleep and rest,
Father will come to thee soon;
Rest, rest, on mother's breast,
Father will come to thee soon;
Father will come to his babe in the nest,
Silver sails all out of the west
Under the silver moon;
Sleep my little one, sleep my pretty one,
Sleep.

Twinkle, Twinkle Little Star

Twinkle, twinkle, little star.
How I wonder what you are.
Up above the world so high,
Like a diamond in the sky,
Twinkle, twinkle, little star,
How I wonder what you are.

Weary travelers in the dark
Thank you for your little spark.
Who could see which path to go,
If you did not twinkle so?
Twinkle, twinkle, little star,
How I wonder what you are.

OLD WORLD TRADITIONS

E ach ethnic group has wonderful lullaby traditions. What are some of yours? These are worth preserving. If you don't know any, ask your parents or grandparents. Every family has songs to pass along.

German:

Schlaf, Kindlein Schlaf

Schlaf, Kindlein, Schlaf!
Dein Vater hüt't die Schaf;
Deine Mutter schüttelt's Bäumelein,
Da fällt herab ein Träumelein.
Schlaf, Kindlein, schlaf.

Sleep Baby Sleep

Sleep, baby, sleep.
Your father tends the sheep.
Your mother shakes a little tree.
Down falls a little dream for thee.
Sleep, baby, sleep.

Spanish:

Palomita Blanca

Palomita blanca
Del piquito azul
Llévame en tus alas
A ver a Jesus.

Si niñita buena
Yo te llevaré
Porque con mamita
Te hay portado bien.

Little White Dove

Little white dove
With the little blue beak
Carry me on your wings
To see Jesus.

Yes, good little girl
I will take you
Because you have been
Good with your mother.

PARENT A CAPPELLA

Nowhere else can you find such an appreciative audience. Infants respond with equal delight whether you're on key or off. They enjoy free verse or familiar rhymes or made-up verse. Whatever your interaction, it can be enhanced by your choosing *(or creating)* a melody and dubbing in a monologue. The following examples can set your own style in motion.

Free-form: *"We are bathing Baby. . . ."*

"This Papa loves you, loves you . . ."

Create words to familiar childhood tunes:

(to the tune of *"Frère Jacques"*)
Time to dress you,
Time to dress you.
Yes it is! Yes it is!
This is how we do it,
This is how we do it.
I love you, I love you.

(to the tune of *"Farmer in the Dell"*)
We change our diaper now.
We change our diaper now.
Hi ho the dair-e-o
We change our diaper now.

PLAYBACK

Tape record your baby's sounds—all of them—the cries and the coos. Actually playing the tape back to your baby can engage and relax your little one. Even playing back a baby's own cries has been known to put a baby to sleep.

The bonus is that you have a record of these early months to listen to together years later.

POM POM PLAY

To encourage visual acuity, to delight and also expose your baby to anticipated behavior, drop large, brightly colored pom poms on your baby's stomach from a height of about three feet. Drop pom poms one at a time, making each drop an event. *("Here it comes. Watch the Pom Pom. Bong! I dropped it on Pat. Let's do it again.")*

Pom pom balls can be bought or made from brightly colored yarns.

PUPPET PLAY

H old a brightly colored puppet or doll so that its face is just above your baby's. Distinctive facial features have greater appeal to babies. Studies also show that babies prefer three-dimensional faces to pictures of faces—yours being the most interesting of all! *(A newborn's focus distance is only eight to twelve inches, yet by three months, your baby has a full adult focus range.)*

You can make darling hand puppet mitts from outgrown baby socks. Cut five finger holes along the toe line. Insert your fingers which will become wiggly "hair." Using a bold, permanent felt marker, mark two big round eyes, a nose, and a smiling mouth on the palm area and you'll have added a new toy to your collection.

Draw a face on one side of a wooden spoon for another instant puppet.

Get your baby's attention by wiggling the puppet. Then provide the dialogue between the infant and the toy to enhance interest: *"Hi, Big Guy. My name's Alex. I need a friend. Will you be my friend? Watch me dance."* Slowly moving the toy from side to side will also entice your baby to watch it.

Play this game lying down on a bed or couch or on the floor next to your baby. You'll save your back from the strain that bending over a crib, carriage or playpen produces.

RATTLES

The first games you play with your baby will probably be with rattles, to distract and engage attention. Be sure that rattles that come with gifts or that you buy aren't breakable and don't have detachable pieces.

Even a newborn can help you work on an adaptation of "Go Fetch." First, put a rattle in the tight, reflexive grasp of a baby. It will be waved briefly— then dropped for you to "Go Fetch." *(This is the elementary version of a game that will continue with children into the teen years. Enjoy this version. It is probably the simplest and most enjoyable.)*

As your baby grows, offer rattles from the left and right, high and low, so that there will be a need to twist slightly to reach them. Use words like, *"Here is your rattle. Can you reach it?"* Encourage reaching by letting the baby have the rattle. Wait, then place the rattle in a different accessible spot.

Variation: Create your own "rattles." Fill several small plastic film canisters with different objects such as rice, cake sparkles, marbles, beans, or bells, for sound variations. Be sure such holders are securely shut even to the extent of gluing the top in place, as every item will be explored by your baby's mouth.

For an older baby, his or her own set of keys—blanks from the hardware store on a strong ring—make great noise and can be cool teethers.

STARBURST

To improve your baby's eye tracking, use one hand to create a "starburst" effect for your child. With your baby lying face up or reclining in an infant seat, move your hand with all your fingers touching, about 12 to 24 inches away from his or her face. Open your fingers quickly, creating a starburst pattern.

Use a sound to coordinate with the burst of motion in your fingers.

Move your hand from side to side as well as closer and closer. End each sequence with your hand gently catching your baby's nose. This will bring smiles and giggles and maybe even a few squeals of delight.

STEADY AS YOU GO

Place your baby, tummy down, on an inflated beach ball. The ball should have sufficient give and not be fully inflated. Holding your baby securely, rock a baby over two months of age, back and forth and from side to side atop the ball. Actually this is a soothing and calming activity for a baby.

STRETCHY, STRETCHY

Help your baby limber up with stretching exercises. Choose a time when you're changing your baby, so diapers don't encumber the stretches. Be sure the room is warm enough if clothes are off.

Holding your baby's hands, cross them over the chest. Then spread the arms wide and out to the sides. Cross them over the chest again. Repeat this movement several times.

Raise one arm up above the ear while the other is stretched down near the waist. Alternate positions of arms.

Bring them over your baby's head together, then down alongside the body, and release them. Repeat each stretch a few times.

Take one of the baby's arms and the opposite leg and bring them together. Stretch them out. Repeat two more times. Do the same stretch with the opposite limbs.

Also move your baby's legs in a lateral motion. Holding by the ankles, place knees together, then spread legs gently side ways touching soles of feet together. Repeat, using the words, "in and out, and in and out."

Variation: Sitting behind your baby who is face down and propped up on a towel, gently bend one knee, then the other, simulating a crawling movement. Just pressing your hands against your baby's feet will make him or her automatically stretch and push forward against your hands.

STROKES FOR LI'L FOLKS

I nfants, after about their first month, usually love a massage. It helps circulation, relieves colic, reduces stress, and increases the sense of well-being. In a warm room, undress your baby, leaving on only a diaper. With clean hands *(no jewelry, please)*, put some oil about the size of a nickel on your palm. Rub your hands together to warm the oil before putting it on your baby. Massage therapists suggest using vegetable-based oils, or massage oils (almond or sesame oil) rather than petroleum-based baby oil.

Arms and Legs: Massage from the shoulder down to the hand, from the thigh down to the foot, alternating hands, sliding down the limb, squeezing and stroking gently but firmly. Alternate from right to left limb.

Head: With the fingertips of both hands, make soft, rhythmic circles on the crown, forehead, and temples. Stroke from the crown along sides of the face. Use thumbs together on the forehead and slide to sides on the head. Make circles on the cheeks, move to the ears, rub, then squeeze lobes gently.

Baby's Back: With your baby lying face down on a comfortable surface or across your knees, stroke down from the shoulders to the buttocks with one hand, while the other hand secures the child's rear. Then go crosswise on the back with both hands from baby's side to side. Finish with tiny "rain drop" finger taps.

Stop if your baby is cranky and massage isn't having a calming effect. Use massage for only the length of time you both find it enjoyable. Don't apply massage when a baby has a full tummy or is very hungry.

TICKLE TIME RHYMES

Many classic nursery rhymes can be used as tickle games as well as rhymes like those below which are specially geared to tickling. Babies learn to anticipate loving tickling. Still parents need to respect their babies and keep a very gentle touch. Tickling is an invasion of personal space, so it's important for you to observe your baby carefully for any sign that he or she doesn't enjoy it. Use your fingers to "creep" over your baby while reciting these favorite rhymes.

This Little Piggy

This little piggy went to market, this little piggy stayed home.
This little piggy had roast beef, this little piggy had none.
And this little piggy cried, "Wee, wee, wee," all the way home.
*(Hold each toe in turn, starting with the big one. On the last
line, tickle or wiggle baby's foot or toe.)*

Round and Round the Garden

Round and round the garden *(Circle the baby's tummy.)*
Goes the teddy bear. One step . . . two steps . . .*(Walk fingers up chest.)*
Tickle under there! *(Tickle the baby under arms or chin.)*

Jelly

Jelly in the bowl, jelly in the bowl. *(Jiggle the baby's tummy.)*
Wiggle, waggle, wiggle, waggle, *(Gently sway baby by the shoulders.)*
Jelly in the bowl. *(Tickle baby.)*

Slowly, Slowly

Slowly, slowly, very slowly *(Walk fingers slowly over baby.)*
Creeps the garden snail.
Slowly, slowly, very slowly
Up the wooden rail.

Quickly, quickly, very quickly *(Run fingers quickly over baby.)*
Runs the little mouse.
Quickly, quickly, very quickly
Round about the house.

Little Mousie

See the little mousie
(Touch index and middle fingers to thumb for "mouse.")
Creeping up the stair *(Creep "mouse" slowly up your baby.)*
Looking for a warm nest. There! Oh! There! Oh! There!
(Find a corner, like the elbow or under chin.)

Caterpillar

"Who's that tickling my back?" said the wall.
(Crawl your fingers across your baby's tickle spots.)
"Me," said a small caterpillar, "I'm learning to crawl."

THE TOOTSIE ROLL

With your little-older baby lying face up on a mat or rug, get on your hands and knees above him or her. Smile and lower your head while you let your baby know you're coming. Say, *"Toot, toot, Tootsie, here I come! I'm going to roll-l-l-l you over!"*

Talking as you approach, very gently nudge your baby with your hands or head until you've rolled your baby over once or twice. You can even use one of baby's large stuffed toys to "do" the rolling.

Reverse sides. You can make sounds as you approach, or keep up a running patter of conversation, letting your baby know what's coming.

TOY TARGET PRACTICE

Babies love to bat and kick at interesting items in their line of vision as their visual acuity matures. Colorful crib mobiles offer this opportunity but so can you by tying colorful balloons *(draw facial features on balloons)*, small soft toys, wiffle balls, and the like with sturdy strings, ribbons, or elastic to a cord stretched across the crib. You can also just hold strung items above or in front of your baby and play together.

Caution: Never leave your baby unattended when playing with items on a string. And never leave such items, which might cause strangulation, loose in a crib or playpen or with a sleeping baby.

WHO DO I SEE?

W hile babies will understand and enjoy mirrors after they are a few months older, you can start to enjoy the magic of reflected familiar faces now. Hold your baby in your arms, with both of you facing a mirror. Smile at your baby, and say, *"There's Leslie, and there's Daddy (Mommy)."* Touch the mirror. Take your baby's hand and touch the faces in the mirror.

Make a happy face and say, *"See the happy face."* Make a sad face and say, *"See the sad face."* Move to the side of the mirror, then back into mirror view. Say, *"Where's Leslie? Where's Daddy (Mommy)?"* when you're both out of view.

Let your baby look in a hand-held mirror. Later, let him or her hold the mirror and watch the changes as the mirror moves back and forth. You can find non-breakable mirrors for babies that can be left or hung in the crib so the baby can play with "company" when alone.

WRIST WATCH

S lip a colored-fabric sweat wrist band or stretchy ponytail holder loosely around your baby's small wrist. As your little one's hands move about in front of his or her face, the moving color will captivate and entertain. Strong contrasting primary colors, including black, are the most eye-catching.

3 TO 6 MONTHS

Between months three and six, babies become active players in their worlds. During this time, babies learn to initiate social exchanges with smiles, coos, and babble. They learn the excitement of mobility and now begin to grasp what was so recently out of reach such as their own feet.

At three months, baby babble all sounds alike; but by four months babies begin to tune in to the subtleties of the language they're hearing.

As delightful as your baby's laughter is, a delicate line separates enjoyment and fear, laughter and tears. When playing a game, laughter serves as a release valve for your baby. That tension can cross over into fear and crying from one moment to the next.

Babies begin to interact as they try to make adults resume games played together. They also realize that people are more varied and interesting than toys—that people make things happen.

Your baby's repertoire of games is growing, and anticipation is becoming an exciting part of these games. Imitation becomes stronger with more variation. Babies begin to clap or bang, once they're shown how. This mimicry becomes more evident in a baby's babble as well. Such imitation becomes a steady source of happy games between you.

3 TO 6 MONTHS

Airplane Baby
Bus Baby Aerobics
Clap Hands, Clap Hands
Fancy Feet
Feature Focus
Give Them Some Lip
In the Beginning
Inflated Egos
Knee Rides
Mimic Me
Peek-A-Boo
Roll Over
So-o-o Big . . .
Song Games
Teaching Opposites
Tick-Tock
Waving Bye Bye
Wax Works
Way High
What a Kick
Words to Sleep By

AIRPLANE BABY

When neck muscles have strengthened and your baby has good control of his or her head, flying feats become sources of delight.

Lie down on the floor, feet flat and knees up. Holding your baby under the arms, raise him or her gently over your head and then back down to your knees. The two of you will add variations in the flight plan as you play this game (*wiggles*—gentle turbulence). Add interest to the trip by providing commentary: *"This is your captain speaking. . . "*

Variation: When you're standing, hold your baby firmly around the chest, face down in a horizontal position. It's time for your baby to take off— gently. Fly a circuit, going around the room and back for a gentle landing. "Start" your airplane with appropriate noises, spread out your baby's arms to become the plane's wings.

As your baby grows older, you can add loops, rolls, spins, stalls, and other aerobic maneuvers. Add only what your "plane" enjoys and seems capable of handling at any one time.

BUS BABY AEROBICS

L ay your baby on his or her back. Sing this song while you help your baby workout, using the suggested motions.

The Bus

The wheels on the bus go round and round
(Roll baby's arms.)
Round and round, round and round.
The wheels on the bus go round and round, all over town.

The people on the bus go up and down
(Baby's arms go up and down.)
Up and down, up and down.
The people on the bus go up and down, all over town.

The wipers on the bus go swish, swish, swish
(Hold baby by the hips and gently roll them back and forth.)
Swish, swish, swish—swish, swish, swish
The wipers on the bus go swish, swish, swish
All over town.

The horn on the bus goes beep, beep, beep. . . .
(Press baby's tummy.)

The ride on the bus goes bump, bump, bump. . . .
(Gently bounce baby.)

CLAP HANDS, CLAP HANDS

Babies love clapping, even before they can connect their own hands. By four or five months, they're old enough to enjoy clapping games. At some time around six months, a very important developmental step occurs—a baby can spontaneously bring both hands together so they touch each other. This is the beginning of coordination between the two sides of the body. *(See page 86 for more clapping games.)*

Pease Porridge Hot

Pease porridge hot, pease porridge cold.
*(Slap hands on knees three times, then together,
then clap baby's hands three times.)*
Pease porridge in the pot, nine days old.
(Alternate clapping hands, then clap baby's hands and knees.)

Some like it hot, some like it cold.
(Repeat first instructions.)
Some like it in the pot, nine days old.
(Repeat second instructions.)

You can play clapping games with babies even before they can play them alone. Show your baby how and when you clap, or hold your baby's hands and help with the clapping.

FANCY FEET

Babies, during these months, discover and are delighted with their feet. Take advantage of their feet fascination by adorning feet with brightly colored—even different colored socks. You can put small hand puppets on baby's feet or take a plain sock and draw a simple face (eyes, nose, mouth) on the top of the sock, facing in the correct direction for your baby to enjoy. Socks aid and abet coordination skills as your baby learns to "catch" his or her toes, a feat much easier to perform with socks on!

When the socks are off, don't forget:

Eeny, Meeny, Miny, Mo

Eeny, meeny, miny, mo
Catch a baby by the toe.
If he (she) hollers,
Let him (her) go.
Eeny, meeny, miny, mo.

You can attach short, colorful ribbons—one to each foot or to different toes.

Encourage your little ones' interest in their fancy feet by lifting them into view, talking about and even tickling their toes.

FEATURE FOCUS

Babies enjoy touching your face and having you touching theirs. Starting around four months, babies begin to look at and touch their own hands. Those parts of the brain that coordinate seeing with touching are now integrating. The following game can help with this development.

Eye Winker

Eye winker, *(Point to eyes.)*
Tom Tinker, *(Point to ears.)*
Nose smeller, *(Point to nose.)*
Mouth eater, *(Point to mouth.)*
Chin chopper, *(Tap chin.)*
Chin chopper, *(Tap chin.)*
Chin chopper, chin. *(Tickle under the chin.)*

First point to your own features, then point to your baby's. Then guide your baby's finger to point to each set of features.

Baby Bye

Baby bye, here's a little fly.
We must watch him, you and I.
There he goes, on his toes,
Over to our baby's nose.

GIVE THEM SOME LIP

Help your baby learn to identify sounds around you by pointing them out.

- "What does the car say?" *"Vroom, mmmm."*

- "What does the birdie say?" *"Chirp, chirp."*

- "What does the wind say?" *"Whoo-o-sh."*

- "What does the puppie say?" *"Woof, woof."*

- "What does the pussy cat say?" *"Meow, meow."*

- "What does the cuckoo say?" *"Cuckoo, cuckoo."*

- "What does Baby say?" *"Mama Mama. Dada Dada."*

Conversations can expand first with the sounds of *"ba-ba, na-na, la-la, ah, ee,"* and *"oo,"* which are fun and easy to imitate. While you make one of these sounds, place your baby's fingers on your lips to feel the vibrations as each sound is made.

Give 'em the old "raspberry!" Make your lips vibrate by noisily puffing air out with force. Babies love to do this, and may, in turn, help you learn how to do it! Babies also like to imitate tongue clicking and kissing noises.

IN THE BEGINNING

I t's never too early to read to your baby. Read whenever you get a chance. Put as much expression into reading anything aloud as you do into reciting nursery rhymes or fairy tales. Your baby will enjoy the sounds and tones of your voice.

Reading is a good tradition to start when your baby is small. Even in these earliest months, take advantage of reading your own books, magazines, and newspapers aloud, so your baby will learn to enjoy the sound of your voice while you keep yourself abreast of the times.

Your repetition helps focus attention on one word at a time—plenty of challenge for a baby. *"Look at the kitty. What does a kitty say? Meooow. Kitty. See the kitty."*

Babies also love rummaging through colorful magazines. Let yours look through *(and rip up)* ones you've finished with. Watch that pages don't get eaten. Avoid newspapers, as the newsprint makes for dirty fingers and faces.

INFLATED EGOS

P lace a baby who is beginning to sit alone, in the center of a small, inflated swimming tube ring. It gives support and cushions side slips.

KNEE RIDES

This favorite childhood tradition has many variations. For a young baby, being held under the arms offers the most support. Hold your baby straddling your leg, facing you. Move forward to the edge of the chair. Lift your heel so the baby gets a good bounce, and recite a riding rhyme.

I Had a Little Pony

I had a little pony
That trotted up and down.
I bridled him, and saddled him
And trotted out of town.

One, Two, Three

One, two, three
(Bounce your baby.)
Baby's on my knee.
Rooster crows
(Crow "cock-a-doodle doo.")
And away she go-o-o-oes!

Jack and Jill

Jack and Jill went up the hill
To fetch a pail of water.
Jack fell down and broke his crown
And Jill came tumbling after.

Humpty Dumpty

Humpty Dumpty sat on a wall.
Humpty Dumpty had a great fall.
All the king's horses, all the king's men,
Couldn't put Humpty together again.
(At the word "fall," let your knees slide down before resuming your bouncing.)

To Market, To Market

To market, to market, to buy a fat pig,
Home again, home again, jiggety-jig.
To market, to market, to buy a fat hog,
Home again, home again, jiggety-jog.
To market, to market to buy a plum bun,
Home again, home again, marketing's done.

MIMIC ME

Imitate the sounds your baby makes. The two of you can have a charming conversation of *"yah-yah-yah-yah."*

Let your child watch how your lips move to make the sounds you're making. Babies will explore several options *("ma-ma-ma," "da- da-da," "o-o-o-o," "ba-ba-ba," "na-na-na")*. Soon you'll be able to take turns being the imitator and the initiator.

Make your tongue visible so your baby can watch its action in producing *"la-la-la-la."* Teaching how the palate also produces sounds like *"ka-ka-ka"* is more difficult, but through mimicry, your baby eventually will discover those sounds, too.

Point out different sounds, such as those of a clock, radio, refrigerator, washing machine, vacuum cleaner, and running water from the faucet.

In later months, mimic your baby's movements. When your baby reaches out, you reach out. Copy lip movements, feet movements, even crawling activity. Your baby will soon catch on to this game and even reverse roles with you.

PEEK-A-BOO

Put your hands in front of your face. Say, *"Where am I?"* Wait about five seconds. Take your hands down and say, *"Peek-a-boo."* You two will develop variations of this game that will be an ongoing bond for months to come.

- Peek through your fingers, with a long, *"Pe-e-e-ek."*

- Cover your baby's head with a towel, blanket, or scarf. Count to three; say, *"Where's Leslie?"* Flip the corner back and say, *"Peek-a-boo!"* And then hug. *(These "scary" games need the reassurance of hugs.)*

- Say, *"Where's Leslie?"* when pulling clothing over the baby's head while dressing.

- You can play peek-a-boo around the corner when first entering the nursery after nap time, or by putting a pillow in front of your face, or you can make a stuffed animal play peek-a-boo.

- You can create rhymes to add to your game.
  "Peek-a-boo! I see you.
  Mommy loves you, Daddy, too!"

The joy your baby expresses in the classic game of peek-a-boo comes from seeing you magically reappear—not yet understanding that you really haven't disappeared at all. That comes later and then the enjoyment comes from understanding the "secret!"

ROLL OVER

A t around six months or sooner, your baby will discover the excitement of rolling over. To help your baby practice, lay him or her along one side of a quilt or blanket. Gently raise the corners of the blanket to help your baby roll from the stomach to the back. Reward with praise, hugs, and kisses.

Very gently roll your baby back and forth on the bed. Repeat the motion if enjoyed. Announce that you're *"rolling out the cookie dough"* and your baby is good enough to *"eat all up."* Gobble your little one up with your lips.

Caution: Never leave a baby alone on a bed or changing table, who will inevitably roll off the one time you do.

SO-O-O BIG. . .

W ith your baby sitting in your lap, hold his or her hands. Ask, *"How big is Dana?"*

Raise your baby's arms over his or her head and answer, *"SO-O-O BIG!"* This game can be repeated several times. Your baby will enjoy revisiting it for months to come, especially when he or she learns to raise arms overhead, without your help.

SONG GAMES

At this age, your baby finds you delightfully entertaining. You'll continue to be the vocal maestro for this game, but in time your baby will take over directing finger traffic. Initially the whole song may be too long for your baby's attention span so limit verses accordingly.

Where Is Thumbkin?

Where is thumbkin, where is thumbkin?
(Put your hands behind your back.)
Here I am, here I am.
(One thumb comes out and is bent up and down to the music. Then the other comes out.)
How are you today, sir?
(First thumb bends up and down.)
Very well, I thank you.
(Second thumb bends up and down.)
Run away, run away.
(One thumb flies away; other thumb flies away.)

Where is pointer, where is pointer?
(Repeat above with first finger.)
Here I am, here I am.
How are you today, sir?
Very well, I thank you,
Run away, run away.

Where is tall man, where is tall man?
(Repeat above with middle finger.)
Here I am, here I am.
How are you today, sir?
Very well, I thank you,
Run away, run away.

Where is ring man, where is ring man?
(Repeat above with ring finger.)
Here I am, here I am.
How are you today, sir?
Very well, I thank you.
Run away, run away.

Where is pinkie, where is pinkie?
(Repeat above with little finger.)
Here I am, here I am.
How are you today, sir?
Very well, I thank you,
Run away, run away.

Where are all the people,
Where are all the people?
(Repeat above with both whole hands.)
Here we are, here we are.
How are you today, sirs?
Very well, we thank you,
Run away, run away.

TEACHING OPPOSITES

Babies are fascinated by changes you control. Take a walk through the house to show your infant the wonder of opposites that you can work.

Open-Close

- Open a door (drawer, cupboard), then close it.
- Using your hands, sing *"Open, shut them; open, shut them. Let your hands go clap. Open, shut them; open, shut them. Now let them make a flap."*

Full-Empty

- Fill a cup (in the bathtub), then empty it.

Up-Down

- Lift "way high," then lower your baby, *"Down we go."*

On-Off

- Turn on a light, then turn it off.
- Put on, then take off, a hat.
- Turn on, then turn off, the water.

Heighten your baby's delight—and thus your own—by expressing surprise at the change: *"Now the light is on. . . . Ooh! Now it's off!"* Light switches offer an endless fascination for babies and can be a wonderful source of entertainment—and distraction when needed.

TICK-TOCK

Another rhyme that little ones enjoy is the sound and motion of a clock, at least the traditional idea of a clock, before the days of quartz watches and digital faces.

Hold your baby upright in front of you under his or her arms with your hands wrapped around the chest. Move your baby from side to side in a pivoting motion, as you say:

Tick Tock, Tick Tock

Tick tock, tick tock
I'm a little cuckoo clock.
Tick tock, tick tock
Now it's almost _____ o'clock!
　　　　　　　　(time of day)
Cuckoo! Cuckoo!
(Lift your baby up high with each "cuckoo.")

And, of course, don't forget to incorporate:

Hickory, Dickory, Dock

Hickory, dickory, dock.
The mouse ran up the clock.
The clock struck ONE!
The mouse ran down,
Hickory, dickory, dock. *(Tic, tock!)*

WAVING BYE BYE

L earning the hand motion of waving good-bye coordinates hand control, the ability to copy behavior and the concept of leaving. Practice waving good-bye to places and toys, as well as to people and pets.

WAX WORKS

A simple toy that will intrigue your baby is one you can make easily. Wrap some crumpled waxed paper in a colorful cotton handkerchief or bandana, tying the ends to secure the paper inside the fabric.

It is easy for your baby to hold it, and the waxed paper inside makes interesting crinkly sounds. Your little one can play with it alone, or together with you. And when the waxed paper goes "flat," just open it, wash the fabric, which has probably been well "mouthed" by now, and put in a fresh wad of noise-making waxed paper.

Variation: Bean bags are easy to make with scraps of fabric and interesting sounding and feeling items (beans, rice, pennies, buttons, old nylons, or sponges) from around the house. Make sure your seams are fool proof *(and baby proof)*!

WAY HIGH

As your baby gains control of his or her head, after three months or so, he or she can start to take to the air. Sit on the floor with your little one in your lap, facing you. Wrap your hands firmly under the baby's arms and around the chest.

"Are you ready to go up in the air?" you ask. *"Here we go now: one, two, three, wheeee!"*

On the count of three, begin lifting the baby up as you roll backwards onto your back. By the time you are lying down, your baby will be "flying high." Enjoy and expand your baby's delight with a running commentary on the trip: *"Jenny's flying high . . . Whee ! Way up in the sky . . ."*

Variation: Let your arms act as an elevator ride. Simply raise and lower your baby in front of you whether you are lying on your back or sitting on a couch. Keep a running monologue on what's happening. *"Jenny's going u-u-u-up the elevator . . . Jenny's coming dow-w-w-wn the elevator."*

This game strengthens back and arm muscles—yours and your baby's! You'll need them to be able to carry your soon-to-be-bigger baby!

WHAT A KICK

Babies love to kick their little legs. Hold a pillow or other toys at your baby's feet as target practice. You can also move a baby's legs in a kicking motion saying, *"Kick, kick, kick, little kid-o!"* It will bring a smile to both your faces. You can sing this ditty while your baby exercises those little limbs.

If You're Happy and You Know It

If you're happy and you know it, kick your feet.
If you're happy and you know it, kick your feet.
If you're happy and you know it
And you really want to show it,
If you're happy and you know it, kick your feet.

With your baby on his or her back, bend both baby's knees up at the same time. Separate baby's legs gently and pull the legs back together again. Now try this activity with the following variation of *"The Hokey Pokey."*

You kick your right (left) leg in.
You kick your right (left) leg out.
You kick your right (left) leg in
     and you shake it all about.
You do the Hokey Pokey
     and you wiggle it around.
That's what it's all about.

WORDS TO SLEEP BY

T hat transition time as your baby prepares to sleep can be a chance for the two of you to create rituals that become soothing for both of you. Just reciting favorite poems or songs (without singing them) every time you put your baby down can create the soothing quiet time that leads to sleep. You might prefer the words of well-known poets, but these classic rhymes are easy to remember.

Sleep, Baby, Sleep

Sleep, baby, sleep.
Your father tends the sheep.
Your mother shakes the
    dreamland tree.
Down falls a little dream
    for thee,
Sleep, baby, sleep.

Come, Let's to Bed

Come, let's to bed,
Says my Sleepyhead;
Tarry a while, says Slow.
Put on the pan, says Greedy Nan,
We'll sup before we go.

Tomorrow Can Wait

Cleaning and scrubbing
    can wait 'til tomorrow
For babies grow up
    we learn to our sorrow.
So quiet down cobwebs
Dust, go to sleep.
I'm rocking my baby
    'Cause babies don't keep.

Come Live with Me and Be My Love

Come live with me and be my love,
And we will all the pleasures prove
That valleys, groves, hills and fields
Woods, or steepy mountain yields.
A gown made of the finest wool,
Which from our pretty lambs we pull,
Fair lined slippers for the cold
With buckles of the purest gold.

Christopher Marlowe

50

6 TO 9 MONTHS

Now a baby's territory begins to expand rapidly. With sitting alone now mastered, most babies begin their drive to mobility from simple scooting to active crawling—though it may begin as a backward motion. In that drive to be upright, babies enjoy being in a standing position.

You'll also notice baby's thinking skills are expanding as well. How objects occupy space is fascinating to babies at this age. Items fitting within each other, being turned over, going under and over other items, being relocated, or transferred from one hand to the other, are all intriguing actions. Emptying and filling containers becomes a fascinating pastime. Spatial relations and toys with moving parts captivate attention. With a baby's increased ability to explore comes an increased awareness of vulnerability. Beginning at six to eight months, separation anxiety begins to surface.

Baby babble can be assertive in demanding play or food. It can be whimpering with the implied need for cuddling. Your language inflection begins to convey the meaning of the words, too. Babies begin to deduce from your inflections what your message is: happy, angry, excited, indifferent. They begin to respond to their own name.

Your entire home is now becoming your baby's research and sensory laboratory. The mouth is used to explore and learn about anything that can be grasped. Now is the time to carefully childproof your environment. Go through it very thoroughly to control dangers such as cords, medicines, cleansers, and plants.

6 TO 9 MONTHS

Action Songs
Ankle Rides
Book Worm
Changing Ways
Do You Like My Hat?
Drop Outs • Face It
Feeling Good
Finger Play
Hands On
Hide 'n Squeak
Jack-in-the-Box
Kitchen Patrol
Off to the Races
One Too Many
Over You Go
Pat-a-Cake
Play Ball
Pull Off My Glasses
Rub-a-Dub Tub
Toes Time
Tracking
Where's Baby?
Wiffle Will
Zoo Basket

ACTION SONGS

Highlight any song with movement, to delight your baby. Here are two to get you started.

Mix a Pancake

Mix a pancake, stir a pancake
(Hold baby and help her or him
make stirring motions.)
Pop it in the pan.
("Pop" baby down onto lap.)

Fry the pancake,
(Rock baby gently from side to side.)
Toss the pancake,
(Lift baby high.)
Catch it if you can.
(Bring baby down again.)

Popcorn, Popcorn

Popcorn, popcorn
Put it in a pan.
(Pouring motion.)
Shake it up, shake it up
(Gently shake baby.)
BAM, BAM, BAM
(Bounce baby down on your lap with each "bam.")

ANKLE RIDES

Parents of babies have the opportunity to develop amazingly strong ankles as their babies get strong enough to move from mere knee rides to ankle rides. You'll need to hold your baby firmly under the arms, until he or she is strong and well-balanced enough so that you can hold only hands. Sit on a straight-backed chair. Cross your legs, and mount your baby on your crossed ankle. Swing your ankle to a rhythmic beat, such as the following

See-Saw

See-saw, Marjorie Daw,
Jackie shall have a new master.
He can't earn but a penny a day,
Because he can't work any faster.

Pop Goes the Weasel

All around the carpenter's bench
The monkey chased the weasel.
The monkey thought it was all in fun,
Pop! Goes the weasel!

Ride a Cock Horse

Ride a cock horse
To Banbury Cross,
To see a fine lady
Upon a white horse.

With rings on her fingers
And bells on her toes,
She shall have music
Wherever she goes.

BOOKWORM

Homemade books are a special delight to your baby and easy to make to expand your library of baby books. These can be as simple as picture collections of favorite things cut from magazines to photos of family members in albums. Actually small albums with magnetic pages are excellent for do-it-yourself baby books.

Make simple "books" by inserting pictures in heavy-weight, self-closing plastic bags you sew together. Or use heavy-duty clear tape to attach pictures to cardboard. The books will be chewed, so choose your materials with care. Keep books to a size that your baby can easily handle, with just one large, bright picture to a page. Postcards and the fronts of old birthday and Christmas cards that are given a protective "laminate" can be held together with yarn running through punch holes.

Make a touch-and-feel book of interesting textures. Include a variety of items, such as ribbons, zippers, yarn, and different kinds of fabric scraps, such as velvet and corduroy. Avoid buttons that may come off and be swallowed.

"Pat" books that include noisemakers concealed between the pages *(and well attached!)* are especially appealing to babies. Inexpensive noisemakers can be purchased at novelty stores.

CHANGING WAYS

When changing your baby, offer a clean powder puff or cotton ball for exploration. Show her or him how to rub it on the tummy, arms, nose, or face. This can give you an opportunity to talk about body parts.

Even putting on shoes becomes an event if you say this poem:

> Shoe the old horse,
> Shoe the old mare;
> But let the little colt
> Go bare, bare, bare.

When you say the last line, the shoe should be tied. Tap the sole of the foot each time you say, *"bare, bare, bare."* Your baby will anticipate the tapping.

DO YOU LIKE MY HAT?

Babies love hats placed on their heads, especially if they can see the results in a mirror. Hang several hats near a mirror, and watch the fun. Babies younger than six months and older than twelve months also enjoy the many variations that "hat play" encourages.

DROP OUTS

The corollary to the mastery of picking something up, is the mastery of dropping something so it disappears from view. Spare yourself a lot of pick up and fetching by turning it into a game. Tie toys to strollers and high chairs *(never cribs or other sleeping areas, please)* with ribbons, yarn, or shoe laces. Your baby can retrieve them by pulling up the string. Your little one will still need your attention and reactions as items are dropped and picked back up.

FACE IT

Help your baby to enjoy face washings—often a bone of contention—by using this bathtub song, *"This is the Way We Wash Our . . . (face; cheeks, nose, lips)"* (to the tune of *"Here We Go Round the Mulberry Bush"*) This can be especially helpful after meal times, when the baby is in a high-chair. Use the cloth to first wipe your own face, then let your baby clean his or her face, one "item" at a time. Use a soft baby wash cloth—not a rough adult-size one—to make it a more pleasant experience.

Or play a game of peek-a-boo with the wash cloth . . . a damp one, naturally! Lay the cloth on your baby's face, rub it around, and lift it off to say *"peek-a-boo!"* This gives you a chance to see when you've completed the cleaning job—and gives you a cooperative happy partner.

FEELING GOOD

 Let your baby feel the different textures and surfaces to be found all around your house. Talk about what you're feeling (smooth, rough, cold, warm, soft, fuzzy). Touch everything from a mirror to the curtains to the chair fabrics. Don't forget to talk about the texture of skin and hair and finger nails, too.

Make a game of feeling different textures by cutting a hole the size of your baby's hand in a box's lid or use an empty tissue box. Place objects that have different "feels" in the box, such as sandpaper, velvet, linoleum scraps, satin, burlap, an emery board, and fur. Rotate the top layer. *(Be certain to watch for any small pieces that might get broken off that are potential choking hazards if put in the mouth.)*

You can also glue some of these different texture pieces down on a large piece of stiff poster board. As your baby touches each texture, make comments on how each piece feels. Or cut 3" x 3" squares of different textures and give each piece one hole-punch in a corner. Then place these pieces on a large round binder ring and you have an easy-to-take-with-you toy.

FINGER PLAY

Finger play songs are engaging fun for children. The words are traditional and often easier to remember when hand movements are learned with them. Rhythms and rhymes capture babies' interest. This "let's pretend" involves them both in the stories and the action.

Eentsy Weentsy Spider

The eenstsy weentsy spider went up the water spout.
(Touch opposite thumbs to index fingers,
* alternate to twist upward.)*
Down came the rain and washed the spider out.
(Wiggle fingers while moving hands down.)
Out came the sun and dried up all the rain.
(Make a big circle with your arms.)
And the eentsy, weentsy spider went up the spout again.
(Alternate thumbs and index fingers again.)

Make finger loops when playing *"Whoops Johnny."* Touch your baby's thumb, then the tip of each finger. Slide down the outside of the ring finger and up the baby finger, while saying *"Whoops, Johnny."* Then retrace your route back to the thumb. Feel free to use your child's own name in the game.

Whoops, Johnny

Johnny, Johnny, Johnny, Johnny,
Whoops! Johnny!
Whoops! Johnny!
Johnny, Johnny, Johnny.

HANDS ON

 Babies enjoy exploring new textures that can go in their mouths too. Place a dab of yogurt, a spoonful of Jell-O, or some smooth peanut butter on your baby's high chair tray and encourage finger painting. *(Be ready for body painting, too!)* Or pour a quarter cup of bread crumbs or oat meal on the tray to rub hands in. Strands of wet, cooked spaghetti on a highchair tray can captivate your baby's attention for a long time.

HIDE 'N SQUEAK

Make one of your baby's toys squeak, then hide it under a blanket while the baby is watching you. Encourage your baby to find the toy, perhaps giving it a tell-tale squeak through the blanket.

You can also encourage understanding the real-though-unseen by covering up a playing radio or audio tape player.

Or hold a small, interesting toy in your hand. Let your baby see it, briefly. Then close your hand. Encourage your baby to find the hidden toy. Clap enthusiastically when it's discovered. Babies are intrigued at this age to learn that things don't disappear forever when they are out of sight.

JACK-IN-THE-BOX

Sit your baby on your lap for this traditional bouncing game.

Jack-in-the-Box

Jack-in-the-Box, you sit so still.
Won't you come out? "Sure I will!"
Jack-in-the-box, hidden away
Pop out now, so we can play!

Jack-in-the-Box, all shut up tight.
Not a breath of air or a ray of light.
How tired he must be, all folded up.
Let's open the lid, and up he'll jump!

You can also squat down and hold your baby with feet on the floor in a partial squat as you recite this poem. Then jump up together at the last line. With a *"one, and a two, and a three,"* you prepare for a big *"Jump!"* as you scoop your baby up high. *(You'll likely tire of this game before your baby does.)*

Or turn it into a finger game where you make two fists with your thumbs tucked in and recite a Jack-in-the-Box rhyme. With the last sentence, pop your thumbs out with an accompanying verbal noise or exclamation.

Variation: Any baby will be captivated by Jack-in-the-Box-type toys and will soon learn to anticipate the excitement of "Jack's" jumping up. But you don't have to own an actual Jack-in-the-Box because you can easily make your own variation using a paper cup and a popsicle stick inserted through the bottom to which you've attached a toy or paper doll drawing that can "jump" up. Also any small toy can "pop out" from behind a chair or over a bannister.

KITCHEN PATROL

P lace a cooking pot upside down on the floor in front of your baby. Encourage your little one to figure out which way is up for the pot and how to get it right-side-up. Then supply a lid that fits and show how it nestles into the pot. That coordination trick will demand practice and concentration.

Babies appreciate an available low drawer or cupboard to call their own where you store safe kitchen items suitable for stacking, banging, and nesting.

OFF TO THE RACES

B oth of you can get a good workout with this romp. Holding your baby in your arms, gallop around the room singing:

Riding on My Pony

Riding on my pony,
My pony, my pony.
Riding on my pony,
Whoa! Whoa! Whoa!
(Pull your pony to a stop with each "Whoa.")

ONE TOO MANY

L et your baby hold a small toy in each hand, then offer a third toy for him or her to grasp. This problem-solving excercise will take practice before your child learns to set one toy down before being able to grasp the third one or to hold two items in one hand.

OVER YOU GO

C ross your knees and sit with your baby on the top leg. Hold onto both of the baby's hands, bouncing him or her to the rhythm. On *"Whoops,"* swing your baby by uncrossing your knees.

Over Leg

Leg over leg
A dog went to Dover
He came to a wall—
Whoops! He jumped over.

PAT-A-CAKE

A After you play the first round of this chilhood classic, it's time to guide your baby's hands to do a verse. You can also play it with your baby's feet, clapping the soles together. Daily repetition makes this one a favorite. Repetition helps baby recognize sounds and eventually realize that certain sounds have a certain meaning. Actions give extra clues to meaning.

Pat-A-Cake

Pat-a-cake, pat-a-cake, baker's man,
(Clap four times.)

Bake me a cake as fast as you can.
(Cup one hand, stir with a finger from the other.)

Pat it, *(Pretend to be kneading it.)*

And prick it, *(As with a fork.)*

And mark it with a "B"
(Trace baby's first initial on your hand.)

And put it in the oven *(Pretend to do so.)*

For Baby and me!
(Point at each of you. Hug time!)

PLAY BALL

Sit across from your baby. Roll a ball back and forth between the two of
you. Provide a running play-by-play of what's happening. *"I roll the ball
to you. And now you roll the ball to me."* Or you may choose to sing these
lyrics, using the tune for *"Farmer in the Dell."* You can also use this chant.

Roll the Ball

We roll the ball, it's rolling.
Now roll it down the track.
We roll it down to Baby,
And Baby rolls it back.

Learning to deliberately let go of a thing happens closer to nine months of
age. Encourage "letting go" by asking for the ball.

Variations: Use a large ball as an excellent enticement for encouraging your
baby to crawl. Or put smaller, brightly colored plastic balls in your baby's
bathwater. They become attractive targets for reaching and batting.

PULL OFF MY GLASSES

If you have expendable sun glasses, babies love to remove Mommy's
(Daddy's) glasses and find their loved one! If you use mirrored sun-
glasses, they offer the additional attraction of allowing your little one to look
at and admire his or her own reflection!

RUB-A-DUB TUB

 Bath time can be a highlight of your baby's day as water play is a source of great fascination. This is a good time to teach the words to another favorite classic:

Rub-a-Dub Dub

Rub-a-dub dub
Three folks in a tub,
And who do you think they be?
A butcher, a baker, a candle maker
And out they go—all three!

Keep a bag of favorite bath toys ready for water play. Good choices are plastic boats, ping-pong balls, plastic glasses or cups, spongy toys or small sponges, and plastic fish. Catching bobbing toys is a powerful feeling of mastery for babies.

Household items like colanders and funnels make great bath toys. Yogurt containers and margarine tubs with holes punctured in them become good sprinklers. Empty plastic bottles with their caps on are great for filling and pouring—and for just bobbing.

Let your baby wash one of the toys as you wash your baby. Pretend to pour shampoo onto the toy and encourage your child to wash the toy. Then help pour the rinse water over the toy before pouring rinse water over your baby's freshly washed hair.

TOES TIME

Babies are fascinated with their toes. Take advantage of this interest. Join in your baby's fun.

Ten Little Tootsies
(to *"Ten Little Indians"*)

One little, two little, three little tootsies.
Four little, five little, six little tootsies.
Seven little, eight little, nine little tootsies
Ten little tootsie toes.

Ten little, nine little, eight little tootsies.
Seven little, six little, five little tootsies.
Four little, three little, two little tootsies.
One little tootsie toe.

Terrific Toes

I know these toes.
I love these toes.
They are a part of me that grows.

Cute and round,
They touch the ground
In the air they kick around.
Quite a sight, without a sound.

TRACKING

In a darkened room, perhaps at bedtime, turn on a flashlight and encourage your little one to track the light moving around the room. This can be a bit hypnotizing and can be a good game to soothe and relax your baby. Make it part of your own sound and light show with soft background music.

WHERE'S BABY?

S ome where between peek-a-boo and hide-and-seek lies this game. Slip a bath towel or a dish towel over your baby's head and say, *"Where's Baby? Where'd you go?"*

Whisk it away immediately and say, *"There you are!"*

This version can gradually increase its coverage time. Count to ten—or later even twenty—pull off the towel yourself. Soon your baby will pick up the gist of the game and will pull off the towel for you. It will be a great source of glee.

You can also play this game with dolls, toys or family pets. They magically disappear under the towel, and then magically appear again upon demand.

Other versions increase in complexity and daring as your baby grows. Get down on the floor and crawl around looking for your baby. Much of the delight comes from your calling out, *"Where's Terry? Where'd you go? Has anyone seen Terry? Are you under here? Behind there?"*

Soon your baby will learn to scoot away to hide in delight as the game begins.

WIFFLE WILL

Find or buy a plastic wiffle ball—one of those with holes punched all around it. Babies love poking fingers into it as their manipulative skills improve. Later as you start playing rolling and catching games with your child the holes make it much easier for him or her to catch and grab the ball.

ZOO BASKET

Assemble all your baby's animals, stuffed or otherwise, in a basket or box. Join your baby lying or sitting on the floor alongside the basket.

Pull out one animal at a time, and talk about it. Tell its name, the sounds it makes, how it walks or flies, and any other information that might appeal to your baby. Then move the animal next to your baby. Encourage your baby to hold the animal and imitate its sounds. Continue this process until all animals are out of the basket.

Push the basket next to your baby and say the name of each animal as you put it back. As your little one's knowledge grows over this period and into the next six months, encourage your child to pick out the animal you ask for. Eventually your child will be able to put the animals away as you decide which one goes in the basket next.

9 TO 12 MONTHS

As you approach the end of your baby's first year, it's hard to believe all the changes that have occurred. Your baby's perceptions now are sharp in both visual and listening skills. As babies move toward the first birthday, they can tell whether an object is upside down, whether it's a teddy bear, a sibling, or a cup. They can tell where a sound originates and recognize family voices. Your baby may imitate your actions, from your unconscious pulling on an ear lobe to the conscious wrinkling of your nose.

Your conversations become more intense with content and variety. You may see imaginative play emerge in pretending. One-year-olds often know how to tease their companions. Social skills are also building. Language development allows a baby to understand and respond to simple commands (*"throw a kiss"*). First words may appear now—or a year from now.

The pincer grasp, whereby a baby has the ability to hold things between the thumb and the finger, is now mastered. The good news is babies enjoy feeding themselves by picking up small items like Cherrios. The bad news is that every small item becomes something fascinating to pick up and place in the mouth. Be watchful.

The battle between growing independence and the need for security continues to require a lot of energy. Babies will grab at spoons while being fed. Crawling, and maybe even walking, create exciting feelings of independence. But you will find "lovies" often acting as a trusting substitute for parental security during exploration or separation.

Spatial relations continue to intrigue babies. While they continue their interest in stacking or filling containers, they often like to explore spaces with their own bodies—be it under chairs, behind a couch, or in a closet.

9 TO 12 MONTHS

Artist-in-Residence
At Attention
Baby Bouncing
Balloon Games • Blanket Fun
Clothespin Drop
Counting On Those Fingers
Creative Stacking
Croquet
Foreign Legions
Funny Face
Globe Trotting
Gotcha • Grannie Play
I Got Rhythm
I'm Pouring Me Out
I See —You See
Let's Clap • Make Rain
Megaphone Magic
Off to the Farm
School Daze
Spilling—Pouring Power
Stair Master • Stuck Up
Tug of War • Toy Tug
Waxed Paper Fun
Write Now
Yank-Y Drooler
Your Very Own Birthday

ARTIST-IN-RESIDENCE

You can use pudding as an edible finger paint. Put a small dollop on a piece of waxed or shelf paper on the highchair tray. Show what fun it is to make designs on the paper—licking your fingers along the way. When the "artwork" is dry, it can be displayed on the refrigerator! *(Remember to use magnets. Use tape only on non-metallic surfaces.)*

AT ATTENTION

Standing is one of the most exciting skillls your baby will be learning now. Encourage a child to pull him or herself upright by placing a favorite toy on a chair *(a sturdy one, please)* as an incentive.

Do understand that when a baby first learns to stand, he or she can not sit down again. You need to be sympathetic to your child's frustration over this and patiently take hold of his or her hands and gently lower your baby to a sitting position, until this downward skill is learned.

Caution: A child who is learning to stand will use anything available to raise him or herself. Be careful of overhanging tableclothes, unstable pieces of furniture and electric cords.

73

BABY BOUNCING

Knee games continue to be enjoyed. In addition to the ones mentioned before, increase your repertoire with this one.

Trot, Trot, Trot

Trot, trot, trot to London.
(Bounce your baby on your knees, facing you.)
Trot, trot, trot to Dover.
Look out, Lynn *(Baby's name.)*
Or you might fall O-VER!
(Tip baby to one side.)
Trot, trot, trot to Boston.
(Knee-bounce baby again.)
Trot, trot, trot to Lynn.
*(Support your baby's waist and neck firmly with
     your hands,)*
Look out, Lynn! Or you might fall IN!

(Open your knees and let your baby "fall" backwards until his or her head is by your ankles. When your baby is used to this game, you can hold onto just the hands instead of giving full support.)

BALLOON GAMES

Add one-fourth cup water to a small balloon and tie it closed with a knot. Show your baby how it changes shape as you squeeze and wiggle it. Let your baby play with it while you supervise. Discover how it bounces when dropped. Roll the balloon around, too.

Balloons can be instant amusement whenever you need some. Keep one in your purse. You can blow it up and your baby will be fascinated watching it soar if you let go of the it without tying it. If you can pull the neck of the balloon while letting air out, your baby will delight in the noises it emits. And a blown-up balloon is always popular.

Caution: Never leave a baby unattended with a balloon, whether inflated or deflated. The balloon, or pieces of it, can be swallowed and obstruct air passages. You can avoid the chance of broken balloon pieces by placing a small inflated one inside a section of nylon panty hose.

BLANKET FUN

Your baby will love blanket rides along the floor, as long as your starts and stops are gentle. A natural time for such rides is on the days you strip beds and your child rides from room to room on the linens or even bath towels. A family room throw blanket can also be used this way.

CLOTHESPIN DROP

Give your baby a handful of clothespins and a plastic jar or bucket. Drop the clothespins from a few inches above the size container. Your child may need help at first. As proficiency increases, vary the containers and the distance to drop. Soon your toddler will be able to stand up and drop the pins in a coffee can *(you'll both enjoy the satisfying clunk that can make!)* or wide-mouth plastic bottle.

If you have non-clip clothespins, show your baby how to slip them onto the rim of a coffee can. This game is great for developing eye-hand coordination.

COUNTING ON THOSE FINGERS

Remember that fingers are for counting. This little rhyme turns learning numbers into a silly game that your baby will love.

One, Two, Three, Four, Five

One, two, three, four, five *(Count on fingers.)*
Once I caught a fish alive. *(Wiggle hand like a fish.)*
Six, seven, eight, nine, ten. *(Count fingers on second hand.)*
Then I let him go again. *(Pretend to throw fish back.)*
Why did I let that fishie go?
Because he bit my finger so! *(Shake hand as though in pain.)*
Which finger did he bite?
This little finger on the right! *(Hold up little finger on right hand.)*

CREATIVE STACKING

Empty food boxes make entertaining blocks to sort, stack, and knock over. Collect cardboard boxes, plastic tubs, egg cartons and any other containers that can provide interesting and easy stacking for your baby. Create your own light-weight blocks from clean, cut-down milk cartons that you cover shut with self-adhesive Con-tac or colored paper. Keep this collection in a low cabinet in the kitchen or even in a laundry basket, for easy access by your child. Spend time together with you stacking and your baby smacking down your towers.

CROQUET

A wooden spoon and ping-pong ball can give you a rousing game of free-form croquet while sitting on the floor. You also can use any other "mallet," like a tongue depressor or cardboard tube, and any other small ball. The object can be to bat the ball wherever it wants to go. Or you can even aspire to hit it between the two of you. Together, you will no doubt develop your own adaptations while you play.

FOREIGN LEGIONS

O ther languages and symbols of other cultures continue to be found among our classic childhood songs. This one seems as American as it is French!

Alouette

Alouette, gentille alouette,	*(Lark, gentle lark)*
Alouette, je te plu-me-rai.	*(Lark, I pinch you)*
Je te plu-me-rai la tête,	*(I pinch your head)*

      (echo) "Je te plu-me-rai la tête"

Et la tête, *(echo)* "et la tête" *(and the head)*

Alouette, *(echo)* "alouette"

Oh,

Alouette, gentille Alouette,

Alouette, je te plu-me-rai.

In each stanza after the first, the words of the preceding verses are repeated in reverse order. The other stanzas, echo, and final refrain include:

le bec	*(mouth, beak)*
le dos,	*(back)*
le cou,	*(neck)*
les yeux,	*(eyes)*
le nez,	*(nose)*
la queue,	*(tail)*

And others are as much fun to learn in other languages as they are in our own. Take for instance, the French and Spanish versions below:

Jack and Jill

Jack and Jill went up the hill
To fetch a pail of water,
Jack fell down and broke his crown
And Jill came tumbling after

(in Spanish)
Jack y Jill subieron la cuesta
Para acarrear el agua
Jack se cayó
Quebró su corona
Jill se vino redando

(in French)
Jean et Jeanne sur la montagne
Un seau d'eau douce chèrcherent;
Jean tomba
la tête se cassa
Jeanne culbuta derrière

Are You Sleeping?

Are you sleeping? Are you sleeping?
Brother John, Brother John,
Morning bells are ringing
Morning bells are ringing,
Ding, dang, dong. Ding, dang, dong.

(in Spanish)
Fray Felipe, Fray Felipe
Duermes tú? Duermes tú?
Suenan las campanas
Suenan las campanas
Din, dan, don. Din, dan, don.

(in French)
Frère Jacques, Frère Jacques
Dormez-vous? Dormez-vous?
Sonnez les matines
Sonnez les matines,
Din, dan, don. Din, dan, don.

FUNNY FACE

Babies delight in mimicking other people. You two can use a mirror to make a delightful game of this developing skill. Each of you can take turns in choosing who mimics the expression—a wrinkled nose, a funny lip pursing, a wink, or a frown. Practice throwing kisses too. Making happy and sad faces helps babies learn that faces can express how people feel.

This little poem is worth capturing on video to save a slice of babyhood.

Wiggles
I wiggle my fingers,
I wiggle my toes.
I wiggle my shoulders,
I wiggle my nose.
Now the wiggles are out of me.
See how still I can be.

GLOBE TROTTING

Invest in a container of bubble blowing soap to entertain and delight your little one. Babies are fascinated by the bubble's colors and ability to float. Watch the smiles of surprise as the bubbles pop when chased and touched.

GOTCHA

This is the reverse of "I'm Gonna Getcha" where your baby is now encouraged to take on your role. Call to your baby, saying, *"Come and get me!"* Be creative by moving under, over, and through various spaces. Cut the ends out of large cardboard boxes so they can be crawled through. When your baby reaches you, pretend to be captured. With big hugs and perhaps a tumble to the floor.

Next, it's time to send the baby off to capture another. *"Go get Daddy!"* He'll soon be tackled by a toddler flinging herself or himself into dad's arms or around his legs.

This game is good for beginning walkers. Help them move and "cruise" by arranging furniture so they can hold on to stationary items to maintain balance. But can be played by active crawlers, too. Just get down on all fours and let your baby give chase.

Variation: This can be expanded into an early version of "Hide and Seek." One parent hides behind a piece of furniture or a door while the other encourages baby to *"Go get 'em!"* Finding the parent is a guarantee of surprise, laughter, and hugs. As your baby gets older, make the hiding places a little harder.

GRANNIE PLAY

Extended family members' names can be brought into play, even in some what stereotyped roles. Babies enjoy the pantomime playfulness of gestures with poems that can be taught to and shared with grandparents.

Grannie's Spectacles

Here are Grandma's spectacles
(*Make circles with thumbs and index fingers placed over eyes.*)
And here is Grandma's hat,
(*Join hands at fingertips and place on top of head.*)
And here's the way she folds her hands
(*Fold hands and place gently on lap.*)
And puts them in her lap.

Here are Grandpa's spectacles
(*Make larger circles with thumbs and index fingers
and place over eyes.*)
And here is Grandpa's hat,
(*Make larger pointed hat, as above.*)
And here's the way he folds his arms
(*Fold arms with vigor.*)
And sits like that!

I GOT RHYTHM

A wooden spoon makes a satisfying sound on pie tins and metal pans. Empty cereal boxes are also good for drumming. Encourage your baby to beat rhythms that you suggest with your voice, such as *"BOOM, ba-ba BOOM, ba-ba BOOM."* Beat to the rhythm of favorite nursery rhymes, too.

Fee Fi Fo Fum

Fee Fi Fo Fum
I smell the smell
of a Tweedledum

Baa Baa Black Sheep

Baa baa black sheep
Have you any wool?
Yes, sir, yes, sir.
Three bags full.

One for my master,
One for my dame,
And one for the little one
Who lives down the lane.

One, Two, Three, Four

One, two, three, four,
Jingle at the cottage door,
Five, six, seven, eight,
Jingle at the cottage gate.

Mary Had a Little Lamb

Mary had a little lamb,
Little lamb, little lamb.
Mary had a little lamb,
Whose fleece was white as snow.

Everywhere that Mary went,
Mary went, Mary went,
Everywhere that Mary went,
The lamb was sure to go.

There's no need to encourage drum practice on your baby's high chair tray. He or she will discover it without your help.

I'M POURING ME OUT

While even a twelve-month-old can't manage this traditional song game alone, it—like others—can be introduced with your demonstrating the moves and then actually helping your child act out the motions by moving his or her limbs and body in the appropriate fashion.

I'm a Little Tea Pot

I'm a little teapot, short and stout,
(While standing, puff yourself up.)

Here is my handle, here is my spout.
(Place left hand on waist, cock your right hand and elbow like a spout.)

When I get all steamed up, I will shout,
(Lean / tip to the left).

Just tip me over and pour me out!
(Then lean to the right to "pour out.")

I SEE—YOU SEE

Help your child's vocabulary development with this simple song game. Pick up or point to an object and sing the following to the tune of *"Frère Jacques"*:

I See Something

I see something, I see something
Used to play, used to play.
It is very round, and it rolls upon the ground.
What is it? What is it? *(A ball!)*

I see something, I see something
Used for drink, used for drink.
It's filled with Timmy's juice, delicious orange juice.
What is it? What is it? *(A cup!)*

Variation: A similar way to add to your baby's vocabulary is to ask, *"Where is . . . ?"* Look around the room and ask, *"Where's Jamy's crib?"* Pause, waiting for your baby to look at the crib. Congratulate him or her and walk over so you can both touch the named object. Choose another object to identify. This game can be played anywhere.

LET'S CLAP

H and-clapping games with your baby are fun because of the added noise created. In addition to just clapping your hands, clap the baby's hands together.

If You're Happy and You Know It

If you're happy and you know it,
Clap your hands *(clap, clap)*.
If you're happy and you know it,
Clap your hands *(clap, clap)*.

If you're happy and you know it,
Then your face will really show it.
If you're happy and you know it,
Clap your hands *(clap, clap)*.

Variation: Add extra verses to your heart's content— tap your head, wave your arms, wiggle fingers, stomp your feet, say huzzah!

Clap Your Hands

Clap your hands, one-two-three.
Play a clapping game with me.
Now your hands have gone away,
(Hide baby's hands under a blanket.)
Find your hands so we can play.

A baby will love watching the hands "go away" and "come back."

MAKE RAIN

Turn a small, clean plastic container into a rain maker by punching holes in it with a pick. Partially fill it with water and give it to your baby to hold up when in a tub. Instead of "taking" a shower, your baby will be making a shower.

Give your child a small plastic or rubber doll to "shower" as a way of an introduction to showering.

A colander produces a short shower, too. It's also useful for capturing and draining toys in the tub.

MEGAPHONE MAGIC

Talk to your baby through a paper tube—an empty tube from paper towels works well. You'll quickly get your baby's attention. Make silly sounds, especially those you've heard your baby already use, like *"ma-ma-ma, ba-ba-ba, da-da-da."*

Give your baby the tube and encourage him or her to imitate those sounds through the tube. If he or she does, echo those sounds back.

OFF TO THE FARM

Through books, visits to petting zoos, and toy miniatures, your little one will learn about the animals to be found on a farm. Children love to learn about animals through the sounds they make, so this song is always a favorite.

Old MacDonald Had a Farm

Old MacDonald had a farm,
    E-I-E-I-O
And on his farm he had some chicks,
    E-I-E-I-O.
With a chick, chick here, and a chick, chick there,
Here a chick, there a chick
Everywhere a chick, chick.
Old MacDonald had a farm.
    E-I-E-I-O.

Remember you can add hand movements as well as sounds of any other barnyard animals such as:

- A Duck—quack, quack; *(flap arms).*
- A Cow—moo, moo; *(milk cow).*
- A Turkey—gobble, gobble *(dip head).*
- A Pig—oink, oink; *(push up tip of nose).*
- A Donkey—ee-aww *(flap hands near ears).*

SCHOOL DAZE

Your baby may not be ready to read, but the rhythms of the *"Alphabet Song"* already will be appealing.

A, B, C . . .

A, b, c, d, e, f, g,
h, i, j, k, l, m, n, o, p,
q, r, s, . . . t, u, v,
w, x, y, and z.

Now I know my ABCs
Tell me what you think of me.

SPILLING-POURING POWER

Your baby can concentrate on developing fine motor skills with those marvelous, tiny hands by the use of intricate maneuvers, such as pouring. You can pour water, toys, or sand. You can count on your baby's helping you clean up after this game. Use small paper cups and Cheerios to let your baby practice pouring. The game can be more intricate if you use three—or even four—cups. Show your baby how to hold the cups and pour their contents from one to another.

STAIR MASTER

Once your little one begins to crawl, any set of stairs becomes a source of fun and fascination. Unfortunately most babies learn to climb up stairs well before they are able to come down them.

Crawling up the stairs with you in a rear safety fall-back position is a fun experience to share. After reaching the top, carry your little one down again to repeat the exercise.

Teach a baby to climb down stairs tummy-down and backwards by reminding him or her to go *"toesies first."* This will require your supervision until mastered.

If your staircase allows, place a safety gate on the third or fourth step up from the bottom so your little one has a small area in which to practice. *(And don't forget to use a second safety gate at the top of the stairs to control access from there.)*

Variation: Climbing skills can be exercised also by climbing over stacked floor cushions, cardboard boxes stuffed with newspapers for strength, or just up and over you.

STUCK UP

Transparent tape provides many fascinating possibilities. Place a short strip on the back of your baby's hand, and let him or her figure out how to remove it. *(Watch that it doesn't get eaten.)* This is also a good trick for keeping a baby engaged during a photo session.

Or give your baby a three-inch strip and show how it adheres to a toy. Pull out a long strip and turn it into a sticky wad.

Or turn a strip sticky-side out and form a loop that will seem to be a handle but will prove sticky. A loop of tape intrigues babies because it is sticky on both sides and can be more easily grabbed to be pulled off.

TUG OF WAR

Tug of war is fun, regardless of the season and the degree of difficulty. You can play this game as soon as your baby can sit up. Give your child one end of a scarf or cloth, while you hold the other. Pull the cloth gently, then wait for your baby to tug at it. When you get a good tug, let go, and tumble over yourself, with enthusiastic sound effects. Encourage your child to do the same and tumble over when he or she pulls hard and you let go.

TOY TUG

With six to twelve-inch strings or ribbons, tie a couple of toys that your baby enjoys playing with to the high chair. After a toy has been swept off the tray—but no longer lands on the floor—help your child learn how to haul it back up. Babies like to pull practically anything attached to a string. Light weight, soft items are easiest.

Tie different colored ribbons to two of your baby's favorite toys such as a pail and a teddy. Put the toys on the floor, with the ribbons within reach of the baby. Ask her or him to give you the bear, then the pail. When your baby has figured out which toy comes when he or she pulls which string, try covering the toys with a cloth. Your baby will then concentrate on learning ribbon placement or color to retrieve the right toy.

Tie short cords *(no longer than two feet long, for safety's sake)* or ribbons to toys that your baby can take for walks around the house. These might be stuffed toys, old jingle circle bracelets, hair rollers, or empty spools. Pull toys that produce a sound when dragged are best. Try two or three empty shoe boxes strung together to carry small toys.

Caution: Don't leave ribboned toys in cribs or playpens during play- or sleeptime, because of entanglement potential.

Variation: Create a toy tug that your little one can ride in. All it takes is a sturdy cardboard box that can support your baby. Tie a rope securely to one end and you can "tug" your child around inside or out!

WAXED PAPER FUN

Show your child how to crumple a sheet of waxed paper into a ball. It provides both sound and grip for an instant toy. Unlike newsprint, it doesn't leave fingers and mouth black. While it's non-toxic, you will still want to monitor a child's inclinations to taste/chew/eat it.

As finger dexterity increases, cut off one strip of waxed paper about five inches wide. Place a safe snack like Cherrios every two to three inches along the length and fold and twist the wax paper between each piece. The challenge is to open and find each snack. This is obviously a game with its own reward.

WRITE NOW

When you sit down with pen and paper, be it to compile a grocery list, write a letter, or pay bills, take the opportunity to be a writing team with your baby. Place paper, possibly taped to a flat surface in front of him or her with a "writing instrument." Some babies are ready to use the non-toxic jumbo crayons at this age, though they'll need to be monitored so the crayons are not eaten.

Hold your baby's hand and guide it on the page—either to make impressions or actual marks. At first your baby may only stab wildly at the paper, but will enjoy sharing the activity with you.

YANK-Y DROOLER

As your baby begins to have good forward motion, place your crawler between two adults sitting on the floor—preferably a carpeted one. One adult encourages the baby, using out stretched arms, to crawl in his or her direction. Once almost there, the other adult gently "yanks" the crawling baby, by legs or torso, back to the starting position.

Teasing language like, *"Oh no, you can't go there"* as you yank your baby back towards you, sets up the game. Repeat as long as your baby enjoys it, but let your little one reach his or her goal if showing signs of frustration.

Variation: For even a walking or older child, being caught by the anklcs and being tumbled to the floor can be great fun, if done gently. Turn your ankle-hold into a sock-only hold as the child squirms to get away. By holding onto only the sock, a child can eventually escape your "grasp" allowing the youngster a victory. The downside of this game, however, can be a drawer full of stretched-out socks!

YOUR VERY OWN BIRTHDAY

Take time to teach the traditional birthday song to your little one in anticipation of that imminent, very special event—the first birthday! While your child probably won't be able to actually sing along, the song will be familiar and enjoyed during your party celebration.

Happy Birthday to You

Happy Birthday to you,
Happy Birthday to you.
Happy Birthday, dear (*baby's name*),
Happy Birthday to you.

Also in advance of the big occasion, help your child learn to mimic the act of blowing in order to participate in the blowing out of that one birthday candle on the cake.

Don't forget to have your camera ready!

Index

OTHER BOOKS BY VICKI LANSKY

- Feed Me I'm Yours
  - The Taming of the CANDY Monster
    - Fat-Proofing Your Child
      - Practical Parenting Tips Yrs 1–5
        - Toilet Training
          - KoKo Bear's New Potty
            - Birthday Parties
              - Welcoming Your
              Second Baby
                - A New Baby at
                  KoKo Bear's House
                  - KoKo Bear's
                    Big Earache
                    - Getting Your
                      Child to Sleep...
                    and Back to Sleep
                      - Trouble-Free Travel
                      with Children
- Baby Proofing Basics • Dear Babysitter Handbook
- Divorce Book for Parents • 101 Ways to Tell Your
Child *I Love You* • 101 Ways to Make Your Child Feel
Special • 101 Ways to Say *I Love You* (*for adults*)
- 101 Ways to be a Special Dad • Kids Cooking
- Microwave Cooking for Kids • Games Babies Play
- ANOTHER USE FOR...101 Common Household Items

To order books or for a free catalog of all Vicki's books,
call 1-800-255-3379 or write *Practical Parenting Books-By-Mail*,
15245 Minnetonka Blvd., Minnetonka, MN 55345

PERFECT FOR THE NIGHT TABLE OF EVERY NEW PARENT!

*For a copy of this 3" x 5" booklet with the words to 22 favorite
lullabies, send $1 and a long, self-addressed stamped envelope
(2 stamps, please) to the above address. Thank you.*